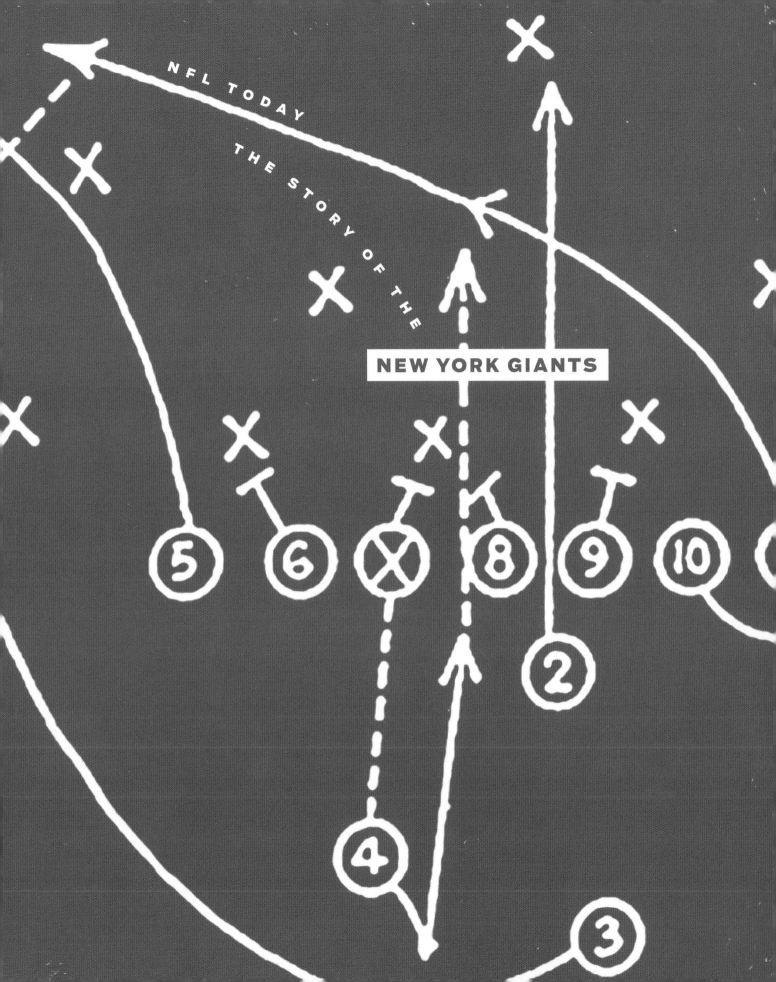

NFL TODAY

THE STORY OF THE

NEW YORK GIANTS

NFL TODAY

THE STORY OF THE NEW YORK GIANTS

JIM WHITING

CREATIVE EDUCATION

PUBLISHED BY CREATIVE EDUCATION
P.O. BOX 227, MANKATO, MINNESOTA 56002
CREATIVE EDUCATION IS AN IMPRINT OF THE CREATIVE COMPANY
WWW.THECREATIVECOMPANY.US

DESIGN AND PRODUCTION BY BLUE DESIGN
ART DIRECTION BY RITA MARSHALL
PRINTED IN THE UNITED STATES OF AMERICA

PHOTOGRAPHS BY CORBIS (BETTMANN, CHRIS
FAYTOK/STAR LEDGER), GETTY IMAGES (AGENCE
FRANCE PRESSE, AL BELLO, PETER BROUILLET,
ROB CARR, BILL CUMMINGS, FOCUS ON SPORT, STU
FORSTER, LARRY FRENCH, GEORGE GOJKOVICH, TOM
HAUCK, KIDWILER COLLECTION/DIAMOND IMAGES,
BEN LIEBENBERG/NFL PHOTOS, EDWIN MAHAN/
NFL, DONALD MIRALLE, NFL PHOTOS, NY DAILY
NEWS ARCHIVE, AL PEREIRA/NEW YORK JETS, EVAN
PINKUS, MIKE POWELL/ALLSPORT, ROBERT RIGER,
GEORGE ROSE, EZRA SHAW, JAMIE SQUIRE, ALLEN
DEAN STEELE/NFL, MATTHEW STOCKMAN, DAMIAN
STROHMEYER/SPORTS ILLUSTRATED, ROB TRINGALI/
SPORTSCHROME, DILIP VISHWANAT, MICHAEL S.
YAMASHITA)

LIBRARY OF CONGRESS CATALOGING-IN-PUBLICATION DATA
WHITING, JIM.
THE STORY OF THE NEW YORK GIANTS / BY JIM WHITING.
P. CM. — (NFL TODAY)
INCLUDES INDEX.
SUMMARY: THE HISTORY OF THE NATIONAL FOOTBALL LEAGUE'S
NEW YORK GIANTS, SURVEYING THE FRANCHISE'S BIGGEST STARS
AND MOST MEMORABLE MOMENTS FROM ITS INAUGURAL SEASON
IN 1925 TO TODAY.
ISBN 978-1-60818-312-8
1. NEW YORK GIANTS (FOOTBALL TEAM)—HISTORY—JUVENILE
LITERATURE. I. TITLE.

GV956.N4W45 2013
796.332'64097471—DC23   2012031651

FIRST EDITION
9 8 7 6 5 4 3 2 1

COVER: DEFENSIVE END JUSTIN TUCK
PAGE 2: DEFENSIVE END JASON PIERRE-PAUL
PAGES 4—5: WIDE RECEIVER HAKEEM NICKS
PAGE 6: RUNNING BACK FRANK GIFFORD

TABLE OF CONTENTS

SIDELINE STORIES

MEET THE GIANTS

NEW YORK CITY IS BIG ENOUGH TO HOUSE TWO NFL FRANCHISES

Big Apple Beginnings

From America's first national census in 1790, New York has been the nation's largest city and, in many ways, its most important. Its location on one of the world's finest natural harbors makes it a center of commerce. One of the city's major thoroughfares, Wall Street, is synonymous with finance. Another noted street, Broadway, has come to represent the world's best theater productions. The city is a fashion trendsetter. And it has long been regarded as the media capital of the United States—if not the world.

Because of the immense media power of "The Big Apple," the fledgling National Football League (NFL) wanted a franchise there. Founded in 1920, the league consisted primarily of midwestern and eastern teams such as the Pottsville (Pennsylvania) Maroons, Rock Island (Illinois) Independents, and Duluth (Minnesota) Eskimos. Games attracted meager crowds at first. Most football fans considered the college game far superior to what the professionals—most of whom made just a few dollars a game and worked full-time at other "real" jobs—put on the field. Few sportswriters took the league seriously.

FULLBACK ALEX WEBSTER SCORED MEMORABLY IN THE 1958 NFL CHAMPIONSHIP GAME

Tim Mara

TEAM FOUNDER, OWNER / GIANTS SEASONS: 1925—59

Tim Mara was probably the only man in New York City with the daring and imagination to make pro football a success in "The Big Apple." Mara, who dropped out of school when he was 13 to support his widowed mother, was a self-made man who wasn't afraid of hard work. Getting people to buy tickets to pro games required a master salesman, and that's what Mara was. "The man was a promotional genius," said local restaurant owner Toots Shor. "You could tell him he had to make germs the most popular thing in town, and he'd find a way. Soon, he'd get everybody in New York absolutely nuts to have germs on their block." But getting people excited about attending Giants games was almost as tough. It took several years before the team turned a profit, and Mara's $500 initial investment ballooned to well over $25,000 with expenses for players' salaries, stadium rental, program printing, uniforms, and equipment. He persevered because he believed in the Giants and saw the team as his family's gift to New York. Mara died in 1959, and his descendants still own and manage the franchise today.

BENNY FRIEDMAN WAS ONE OF THE NFL'S FIRST GREAT PASSERS

In 1925, league president Joe Carr offered New York businessman Tim Mara the opportunity to buy a franchise for $500, hoping to increase the league's exposure. It was a huge gamble on Mara's part. No one knew if a pro team would make money. But the price tag seemed too good for Mara to pass up. "I figured that even an empty store in New York City was worth more than $500," he said. The team played its first games in the Polo Grounds, the home of major league baseball's New York Giants. Accordingly, Mara called his club the Giants.

The Giants were hardly an instant hit. During their first season, Mara and his two sons (ages 17 and 9), the team's entire staff, gave away almost as many tickets as they sold so that the stands wouldn't be empty. New York governor Al Smith, a friend of Mara's, said, "This pro football will never amount to anything. Get rid of that team."

The Giants started out 0–3 before finding the winning touch, finishing their first campaign with an 8–4 record. By far the most important game was against the Chicago Bears on December 6. Bears owner/ player George Halas had signed star running back Red Grange the day after Grange had played his final collegiate game. The Bears began a tour that capitalized on the immense national prestige of Grange, an athlete so famous he was a household name. Although the Giants lost 19–7, they won at the box office. Seventy-three thousand fans packed the Polo Grounds, and, more important from the league's point of view, this included more than 100 sportswriters. Many people believe that game—and the publicity it generated—saved pro football in the U.S. Mara thought so. "My worries are over," he told a friend.

Two years later, the Giants earned their first NFL title with an 11–1–1 record. That team featured a defense that recorded 10 shutouts and yielded only 20 total points, an all-time NFL record. It featured three giant-sized tackles (each weighed nearly 250 pounds) and future Hall-of-Famers—Pete Henry, Cal Hubbard, and Steve Owen.

The following year, the Giants stumbled to a 4–7–2 record. Mara then bought the entire Detroit Wolverines team for $3,500 to obtain the rights to its star quarterback, Benny Friedman. Regarded as the NFL's first great passer, Friedman led the league in both passing touchdowns (9) and rushing touchdowns (6) in 1928, the first—and still only—time that feat has been accomplished. "Benny revolutionized football," said George Halas. "He forced the defenses out of the dark ages."

Friedman worked similar magic for New York in 1929, throwing an NFL-record 20 touchdown passes and leading the team to a 13–1–1 record that marked the second-greatest swing in victories—4 to 13—from one season to the next in NFL history. The lone loss was to the undefeated Green Bay Packers, dropping the Giants to second. New York came in second again in 1930, as the Packers had a better winning percentage, going 10–3 (.769) to the Giants' 13–4 (.765).

Unfortunately, Friedman suffered a severe knee injury in 1931. That same year, Mara appointed Owen as player-coach. Owen would remain the Giants' head coach for 23 years. The club also signed versatile lineman Mel Hein from Washington State University. Hein played virtually every minute of every game for 15 years, as center on offense and linebacker on defense. "In all that time, I can count on the fingers of one hand the mistakes he made," said Coach Owen.

Sneaking to Victory

When the Giants took on the Chicago Bears in the 1934 NFL Championship Game, they were really battling two opponents: the Bears and the ice-covered field of the Polo Grounds. Following four days of rain and a sudden drop in temperature to 0 °F, the field was nearly as slippery as a hockey rink. Giants captain and end Ray Flaherty suggested that his teammates trade in their football cleats for sneakers, and an equipment manager was sent to a nearby college to bring back as many pairs of basketball shoes as he could find. He returned by halftime, with the Giants trailing 10–3. The players donned the sneakers and returned to the field for the second half. When Bears coach George Halas noticed the shoe change, he told his players to step on the Giants' toes. But the suddenly sure-footed "Jints" easily outran their opponents and raced to a 30–13 victory to capture their second league title. "The effect of the new footwear was magical," wrote one New York reporter. The 1934 title contest has gone down in NFL history as "The Sneakers Game."

THE GIANTS DEFEATED THE CHICAGO BEARS TO WIN THEIR SECOND LEAGUE TITLE

GIANTS STARS FRANK GIFFORD, RAY BECK, CHARLIE CONERLY, AND ALEX WEBSTER

Led by Hein, halfback Ed Danowski, and two-way back Alphonse "Tuffy" Leemans, Owen's teams captured eight division titles from 1933 to 1946 and took home championship trophies in 1934 and 1938.

Fans were shocked in 1947 and 1948 when the club posted back-to-back losing seasons. The team returned to its winning ways in the early 1950s, led by quarterback Charlie Conerly, who began setting team passing records. But the Giants consistently finished behind the Cleveland Browns in their conference and did not reach the postseason again until 1956. By that time, Coach Owen had retired and been replaced by Jim Lee Howell.

Mel Hein

CENTER, LINEBACKER / GIANTS SEASONS: 1931–45 / HEIGHT: 6-FOOT-2 / WEIGHT: 225 POUNDS

Mel Hein was an unmovable blocker at center on offense and a devastating tackler at linebacker on defense. He was on the field for 60 minutes of every game during his 15-year career with the Giants. Defenders who attempted to bull past him often found themselves flat on the ground. On defense, Hein pioneered new methods for covering passes and jamming receivers at the line of scrimmage. "He was impervious to injuries," said former Giants owner Wellington Mara. "I heard him call an injury timeout only once, and that was late in his career when he was kicked in the nose in a pileup by one of our own players." Hein nearly missed wearing Giants blue. After his college days, he wrote to several NFL teams offering his services. The Providence Steam Roller offered him $135 a game. Hein signed the contract and mailed it. The next day, he received a Giants contract for $150. He telegraphed the Providence post-master to stop delivery of the first contract. Although that violated postal regulations, the postmaster did as Hein asked. Hein was in the first class elected to the Pro Football Hall of Fame in 1963.

Summerall's Snowy Score

In the last regular-season game of 1958, the Giants faced the Cleveland Browns in a driving snowstorm at Yankee Stadium, needing a win to force a playoff with the Browns for the division title. A tie or Giants loss would put Cleveland into the NFL Championship Game against the Baltimore Colts. The teams skidded and pounded their way to a 10–10 tie late in the fourth quarter. With two minutes remaining, the Giants faced a 4th-down-and-10 situation somewhere across the 50-yard line. (No one could see the yard markers under the snow.) Coach Jim Lee Howell shocked nearly everyone by sending in kicker Pat Summerall (pictured) to attempt a long field goal. "I couldn't believe Jim Lee was asking me to do that," recalled Summerall. "It was a bad field, and it was so unrealistic." But Summerall put his full foot into the kick—which started out wide to the left, then curved inside the uprights for the win. Thanks to Summerall's miraculous kick, the Giants were able to make NFL history two weeks later when they took on the Colts in "The Greatest Game Ever Played."

The Greatest Game and Beyond

Howell inherited a solid nucleus that included Conerly, running back Frank Gifford, and offensive tackle Roosevelt Brown. He traded for fullback Alex Webster and defensive end Andy Robustelli and drafted linebacker Sam Huff. These players formed the core of the Giants team that celebrated its move to Yankee Stadium in 1956 by defeating the Bears 47–7 to win the NFL championship. Playing on a frozen field, the Giants wore sneakers rather than cleats—echoing a virtually identical situation 22 years earlier.

Two years later, New York battled the Baltimore Colts for the championship in a contest that has been called "The Greatest Game Ever Played." It featured 17 future members of the Pro Football Hall of Fame. More people than ever tuned into the game on television.

The drama-packed contest was the first NFL Championship

ROOKIE DON MAYNARD RETURNED PUNTS FOR THE GIANTS BEFORE MOVING TO THE JETS

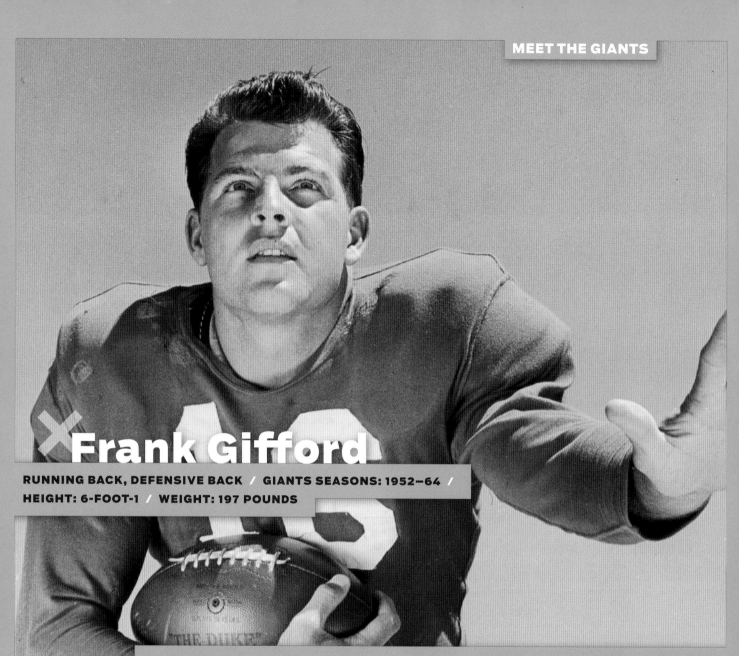

Frank Gifford

RUNNING BACK, DEFENSIVE BACK / GIANTS SEASONS: 1952–64 /
HEIGHT: 6-FOOT-1 / WEIGHT: 197 POUNDS

Frank Gifford had it all—great looks; a powerful physique; an outgoing personality; and outstanding talent as a runner, passer, pass receiver, and defensive back. "Frank was the body and soul of our team," said Giants coach Jim Lee Howell. "He was the player we went to in the clutch." The Giants' top draft pick in 1952, Gifford would impress New York fans with his all-around great play for more than a decade and still holds the team record for touchdowns scored (78). Gifford's best year came in 1956, when he was named the NFL's Most Valuable Player (MVP) and led the Giants to their first NFL title in 18 years. That year, Gifford ranked fifth in the league in rushing and third in pass receiving, threw two touchdown passes, and scored nine other touchdowns. Although not an especially fast runner, Gifford could quickly spot any opening in the defense and burst through the hole with amazing quickness. He played in eight Pro Bowls and was inducted into the Hall of Fame in 1977. Following his football career, Gifford remained in the public spotlight as a television sports commentator and program host.

"It was the beginning for the NFL."

PETE ROZELLE ON THE 1958
CHAMPIONSHIP GAME BETWEEN
THE GIANTS AND THE COLTS

Game decided in sudden-death overtime. The Colts tied the game late in the fourth quarter and eked out a 23–17 win six minutes into the extra session. From then on, pro football was the country's most popular televised sport. "We didn't know it at the time," NFL commissioner Pete Rozelle later said, "but it was the beginning for the NFL. From that game forward, our fan base grew and grew. We owe both franchises a huge debt."

The Giants and Colts faced off for the league championship following the 1959 season, with Baltimore staging a fourth-quarter comeback to again end New York's title hopes. The Giants underwent a changing of the guard in the early 1960s. Howell retired, and assistant coach Allie Sherman replaced him. Sherman revamped the offense by trading with San Francisco for 35-year-old quarterback Y. A. Tittle, who found a new lease on life in New York. "The Old Man" led the Giants to three straight Eastern Conference titles between 1961 and 1963, though the club came up short in the NFL Championship Game each time.

After that, the Giants fell apart. The club won just two games in 1964 and one in 1966. Throughout the rest of the 1960s and '70s, the Giants shuffled through four coaches and five starting quarterbacks, played in four different stadiums, and put together just two winning seasons. The Giants featured several outstanding offensive players during those down years, including scrambling quarterback Fran Tarkenton, tight end Bob Tucker, and running back Ron Johnson. Yet the defense was in shambles. The offense could not put up enough points to offset the porous defense.

To add to the turmoil, the Giants found themselves homeless in 1973 when the Yankees renovated Yankee Stadium and used it for baseball only. So, the Giants began building their own stadium in the Meadowlands in nearby New Jersey. While the stadium was under construction, they played home games 80 miles from New York at the Yale Bowl in New Haven, Connecticut, for two years and shared Shea Stadium with the New York Jets in 1975. Even when the club finally moved into Giants Stadium in 1976, it continued to struggle.

The Giants' prospects began improving when George Young, who had built successful teams in Baltimore and Miami, came on board in 1979 as general manager. Fans questioned his first big move: selecting Phil Simms, an unknown quarterback from Morehead State University in Kentucky, as the

Miracle at the Meadowlands

The Giants lost many more games than they won in the 1970s, but no loss was more devastating than the one to the rival Philadelphia Eagles in November 1978. Amazingly, that terrible loss would prove to be the impetus for turning the team around. With just 31 seconds left in the game, the Giants were leading the Eagles 17–12. Quarterback Joe Pisarcik needed only to take a knee to run out the clock and break the team's latest losing streak. But that isn't what happened. Instead, the Giants' offensive coordinator sent in a play calling for a handoff to running back Larry Csonka. Pisarcik took the snap and reached the ball out toward Csonka—too low. It glanced off Csonka's knee for a fumble that was scooped up by Eagles defensive back Herman Edwards and returned for a touchdown and a 19–17 Eagles win. New York sportswriters sarcastically began calling the play the "Miracle at the Meadowlands." After the loss, several Giants coaches were fired, and a shakeup began in New York that eventually led the Giants back to the top of the NFL.

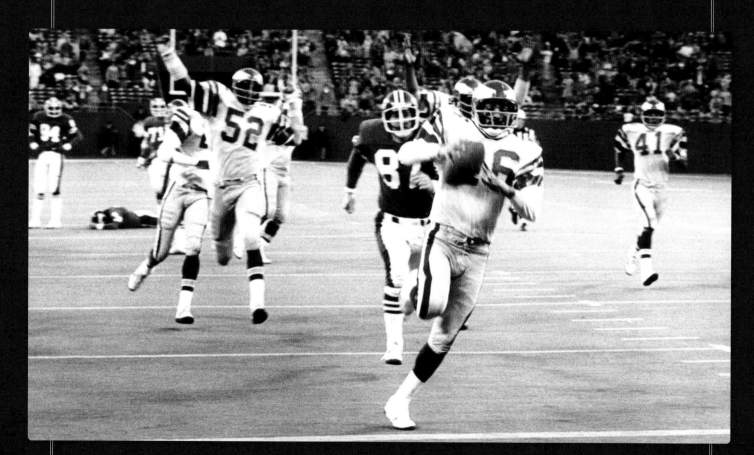

AGONIZED GIANTS PLAYERS WATCHED AS THE EAGLES RAN AWAY TO VICTORY

team's top pick in the 1979 NFL Draft. New York newspaper headlines read: "Phil Who?"

During the next 15 years, Simms answered that question, as fans came to appreciate his talent, courage, and ability to perform in the clutch. Before he retired, Simms would set nearly every Giants passing record. His arrival signaled the start of the franchise's return to respectability. But it was Young's top draft choice in 1981—linebacker Lawrence Taylor—who really transformed the Giants into one of the NFL's most exciting and feared teams.

Taylor helped revolutionize the position of outside linebacker with his speed, anticipation, and aggressiveness. "The ability he had—I still think back to how amazing it was to watch him on film," said fellow Giants linebacker Brad Van Pelt. "He was actually stepping right with the snap of the ball. While everybody else was still at a standstill, he was moving toward the ball—that's amazing."

Playing under new head coach Bill Parcells, Simms directed the offense, and Taylor headed up a defense that propelled the Giants into the playoffs in 1984 and 1985. The Giants were even better in 1986, finishing with a 14–2 record. Taylor was named the NFL's Most Valuable Player (MVP) that year, and running back Joe Morris and tight end Mark Bavaro emerged as offensive stars.

In the postseason, the Giants crushed San Francisco and the Washington Redskins to reach Super

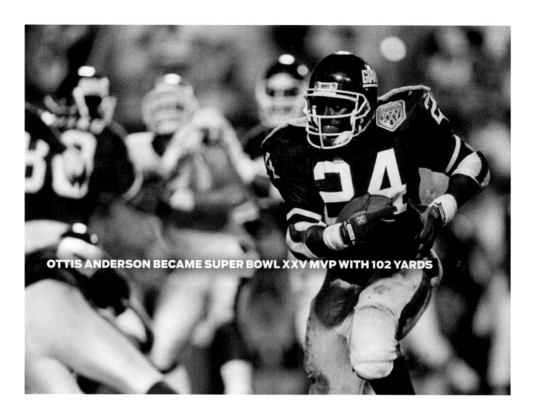

OTTIS ANDERSON BECAME SUPER BOWL XXV MVP WITH 102 YARDS

Bowl XXI opposite the Denver Broncos. In that championship clash, Simms completed a remarkable 22 of 25 passes (a Super Bowl-record 88 percent) to lead New York to a 39–20 victory and its first NFL championship in 30 years.

Coach Parcells's crew made another championship drive in 1990. With running back Ottis Anderson following his massive blockers, the Giants ground down their opponents that year. They started the season with 10 straight victories. After dropping two of the next three games, the team suffered an even greater loss when Simms went down with a season-ending foot injury. Backup quarterback Jeff Hostetler led the Giants to victories in their last two regular-season games. The team's defense took over in the playoffs, as the Giants dominated Chicago and topped San Francisco to earn a berth in Super Bowl XXV against the Buffalo Bills.

Using their running game to perfection, the Giants controlled the ball and the clock. Still, they held only a 20–19 lead as the Bills lined up for a potential game-winning field goal in the closing seconds. When the kick by Buffalo's Scott Norwood sailed wide right, the Giants claimed their sixth NFL championship.

Phil Simms's Biggest Play

Late in the 1986 season, the Giants were in a three-way dogfight with Chicago and Washington for the NFC's best record and home-field advantage throughout the playoffs. With every game crucial, New York trailed the Minnesota Vikings by a point with barely a minute remaining. The Giants faced a 4th-down-and-17 situation on their own 48-yard line. As he took the snap and looked downfield, quarterback Phil Simms saw that his primary receiver was covered. A moment later, he threw toward wideout Bobby Johnson. "I just ran to the first-down marker and stopped," Johnson said. "And when I turned, the ball was there." The resulting first down kept the drive alive, and Raul Allegre kicked a game-winning, 33-yard field goal with 12 seconds left. "It's my favorite game in my career, because it's everything I always wanted to be as a player," Simms said years later. "I wanted to be tough, making big throws, immune to pressure." The Giants went on to secure home-field advantage and advanced to the Super Bowl, where they defeated Denver 39–20 and finished 17–2, their best record ever.

BEFORE ELI MANNING ARRIVED, PHIL SIMMS HELD MOST OF THE GIANTS' PASSING RECORDS

JIM FASSEL FIRED UP HIS GIANTS PLAYERS FOR SEVEN SEASONS

Beasts of the East

New York went into a decline in the early 1990s. When both Simms and Taylor hung up their jerseys at the end of the 1993 season, it signaled the ending of another golden era in the Big Apple.

After going 6–10 in 1996, the Giants hired offensive specialist Jim Fassel as head coach. Fassel's first squad got off to a 1–3 start, and fans booed loudly. But Fassel refused to make drastic changes. "The little red panic button is always there if you want to reach up and push it," he said. "But I would have lost [the players] right then if I started to make wholesale changes.... Everything I had told them about being consistent and staying the course would have gone out the window."

Boos quickly turned to cheers as Fassel's new offensive system began to click. The team finished the 1997 season 10–5–1. In just one year, Coach Fassel had helped lift the team from last place to first in the National Football Conference (NFC) East Division.

Fassel's Giants soon were ready for another championship run. Behind strong-armed

DEFENSIVE END/TACKLE KEITH HAMILTON ADDED CRUSHING FORCE TO THE GIANTS

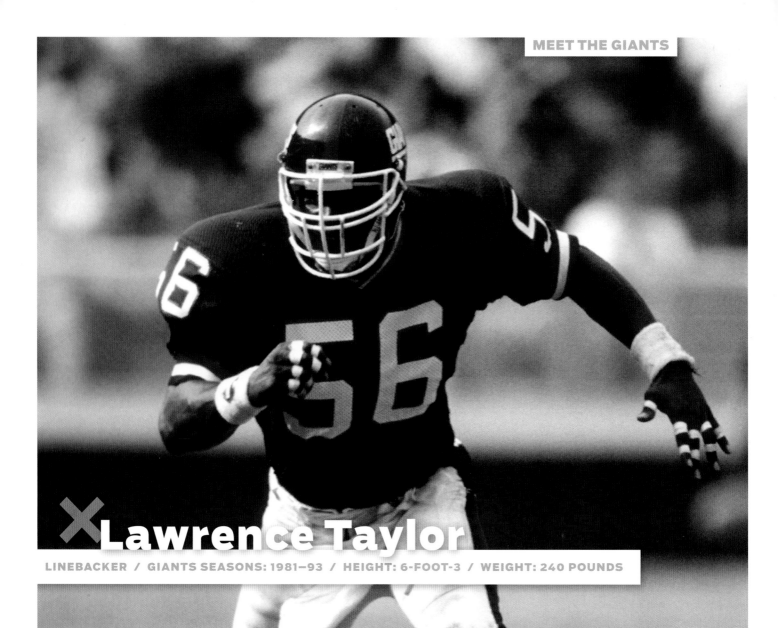

Lawrence Taylor

LINEBACKER / GIANTS SEASONS: 1981–93 / HEIGHT: 6-FOOT-3 / WEIGHT: 240 POUNDS

No defensive player has ever disrupted an opponent's offense more completely than Lawrence Taylor. When "L. T." lined up at his outside linebacker position, poised to charge the quarterback or take on a receiver, offensive linemen forgot counts and often jumped offsides. Quarterbacks fidgeted nervously and dropped back quicker than usual, hoping to avoid a sack. Even when he was triple-teamed by blockers, Taylor often found a way to break up the play. "If there was ever a Superman in the NFL," said former Washington Redskins quarterback Joe Theismann, "I think he wore number 56 for the Giants." Taylor had not only great talent but also an intense work ethic. "Lawrence Taylor brought energy to the team, in games and in practice, and it rubbed off on all the other guys," said New York quarterback Phil Simms. "Players around him would say, 'Hey, I got to try harder, otherwise I'll look absolutely horrific out there playing next to Lawrence Taylor.'" L. T. was a Pro Bowl selection for 10 consecutive years and was named league MVP in 1986. He was inducted into the Hall of Fame in 1999.

JEREMY SHOCKEY WAS NAMED TO THE PRO BOWL FOUR TIMES

quarterback Kerry Collins and elusive running back Tiki Barber on offense and overpowering end Michael Strahan on defense, the Giants finished the 2000 season with five straight victories to capture another division title. Barber recorded the first of six 1,000-yard rushing seasons with the Giants, while Strahan built on his reputation as one of the league's best at chasing down quarterbacks.

The Giants added two more wins in the playoffs to capture the NFC crown and reach the Super Bowl against the Baltimore Ravens. However, New York's exciting run stopped there, as the fierce Ravens defense shut them down, 34–7. The Giants contributed to their own demise by committing 5 turnovers. "That's what hurts so bad, because we didn't play well," said offensive tackle Lomas Brown. "I'm just really disappointed to play this big of a game and not play well."

In the 2002 NFL Draft, the Giants added tight end Jeremy Shockey. The rookie was an instant star, leading all NFL tight ends in receptions (74) and receiving yards (894). Known for his fiery personality, he was also the league's "trash-talking" leader. Shockey's ability to catch passes and carry defenders on his back for big gains forced opponents to double-team him, which helped open up the field for other

receivers such as speedsters Ike Hilliard and Amani Toomer. The result was a 10–6 record and another trip to the playoffs for New York.

The 2003 season turned out to be a mixed blessing in New York. On the negative side, the Giants played poorly for most of the year, finishing last in their division and costing Coach Fassel his job. He was replaced by Tom Coughlin, a former Giants assistant. On the positive side, the Giants' poor record "earned" them the fourth pick in the NFL Draft. They traded that selection and several other draft choices to the San Diego Chargers to obtain the top pick, University of Mississippi quarterback Eli Manning. Manning, whose father Archie and brother Peyton were also star NFL quarterbacks, arrived in New

TIKI BARBER BECAME THE GIANTS' ALL-TIME LEADING RUSHER BY 2007

The Manning Bowl

In 2006, national media had a field day with the "Manning Bowl," which pitted Eli Manning's Giants against Peyton Manning's Indianapolis Colts in the first-ever NFL game with brothers quarterbacking opposing teams. Because of their five-year age difference, it also marked the first time the Manning brothers had competed against each other in any organized sport. Peyton joked that "my mom is going to pull for both of us to stay healthy, and my dad is going to pull for a lot of offense." Both parents were happy. The brothers went uninjured, and Indianapolis managed a 26–21 victory. The difference in the game was two Eli turnovers—an interception and a fumble. A New York writer grumbled that the game "was probably nowhere near a fair fight. Peyton was coming off his third consecutive All-Pro season and already had two MVP awards in his pocket. Eli, on the other hand, was entering just his second full season as the Giants' starter." In Manning Bowl II, played four years later, a more seasoned Eli and his team were overwhelmed 38–14. Yet by 2013, Eli owned two Super Bowl rings to his older brother's one.

ELI MANNING HAS HAD LITTLE TROUBLE KEEPING UP WITH HIS BIG BROTHER

IKE HILLIARD WAS A RELIABLE TARGET FOR GIANTS QUARTERBACKS

York with great fanfare. Headlines read "Eli's Coming" in New York papers, echoing the title of a hit song from the 1960s.

Coach Coughlin originally planned for Manning to watch from the sidelines his first year. But when the Giants struggled offensively in the middle of the season, Manning became the starter. Nervous and inexperienced, he made a lot of mistakes.

anning performed inconsistently the next two seasons as well. "He throws off the wrong foot," some experts said. "He doesn't read defenses well and rushes his passes," others noted. But nearly everyone believed he had a special talent that would eventually emerge. "He makes decisive decisions … and he gets rid of the ball. You love to see that in a young quarterback," said Hall of Fame quarterback Dan Marino.

Manning weathered the criticism and began asserting his leadership on the field, especially in clutch, late-game situations. Behind his passing and the outstanding running and receiving of Barber, the Giants reached the playoffs in 2005 and 2006. But they failed to win a postseason contest either year.

Two More Titles

Giants fans were nervous as the 2007 season began. Barber had retired, and the offensive burden now fell more squarely on Manning's shoulders. When the team lost its first two games badly and barely won its third, fans were certain that 2007 would be a lost season in New York. Yet the club rebounded, finishing the season 10–6 to claim a Wild Card berth in the playoffs.

That was only the beginning. In three postseason road games, Manning displayed a confidence he had never shown before. Alternating passes to receivers such as Toomer and Plaxico Burress and handoffs to running backs Brandon Jacobs and Ahmad Bradshaw, Manning directed an offense that suddenly seemed unstoppable. The high point was the NFC Championship Game, in which Manning outplayed future Hall-of-Famer Brett Favre of the Green Bay Packers at frigid Lambeau Field to lead the Giants to Super Bowl XLII.

The Giants were heavy underdogs to the New England Patriots, who had won all 16 of their regular-season games, plus 2 playoff games, and were determined to become

PLAXICO BURRESS MADE THE WINNING TOUCHDOWN CATCH IN SUPER BOWL XLII

MICHAEL STRAHAN FELLED MANY AN OPPOSING QUARTERBACK OVER HIS CAREER

Phil Simms

QUARTERBACK / GIANTS SEASONS: 1979–93 / HEIGHT: 6-FOOT-3 / WEIGHT: 216 POUNDS

When Phil Simms joined the Giants as a surprise first-round draft pick in 1979, the team had endured 6 straight losing seasons and had not appeared in a postseason game in 15 years. The losing continued during Simms's first five seasons in New York, as he suffered through growing pains learning how to be an NFL quarterback and real pains from a variety of injuries. Then, beginning in 1984, Simms took control of the team's offense, leading the Giants to three straight playoff berths and, finally, a Super Bowl championship in 1986, earning MVP honors. "Phil Simms started to show us his confidence—the way he carried himself in the locker room, the way he carried himself on the field," said Giants linebacker Lawrence Taylor, "and we all became confident that he was going to get the job done." Known for his fiery, competitive spirit, Simms played all 15 of his pro seasons in New York and still holds more than half of the team's passing records. His number 11 jersey was retired in 1995.

the first NFL team to go 19–0 in a season. But the Giants unveiled an aggressive, blitzing defense led by Strahan and fellow end Osi Umenyiora that held the high-powered Patriots in check.

Even after New England took a 14–10 lead with less than three minutes remaining, the Giants weren't ready to concede. Manning directed a scoring drive that featured one of the most exciting plays in Super Bowl history. He ducked and spun his way out of the grasp of several tacklers and completed a long pass to wide receiver David Tyree to keep the drive alive. Then Manning hooked up with Burress for the winning score. "We shocked the world but not ourselves," said linebacker Antonio Pierce.

Some experts thought New York's 2007 title had been a

BRANDON JACOBS SCORED A CAREER-HIGH 15 TOUCHDOWNS IN 2008

fluke, but the 2008 Giants proved they were the real deal by going 12–4 and running away with the NFC East crown. There would not be another Super Bowl parade in New York, however. The Giants ran into a red-hot Philadelphia Eagles team in the first round of the playoffs and lost, 23–11.

The following year, the Giants appeared to pick up where they had left off, opening the season 5–0. But a defeat to the New Orleans Saints started a four-game losing streak, and New York limped to an 8–8 final mark that kept it out of the playoffs for the first time in five years.

The 2010 season featured the opening of the team's new home, the 82,566-seat New Meadowlands Stadium (later renamed MetLife Stadium), the NFL's largest venue in terms of permanent seating capacity. Although the team finished 10–6 in its new surroundings, it missed the postseason.

ith Eli Manning entering the prime years of his career, Giants management wanted to ensure he had plenty of reliable targets. In 2009, they made wide receiver Hakeem Nicks their top draft choice. The following year, they added a pair of undrafted free agents: wide receiver Victor Cruz and tight end Jake Ballard. By 2011, all three were making major contributions. On the other side of the ball, young defensive end Jason Pierre-Paul also emerged as a force, earning NFL All-Pro honors in 2011. "He's had a phenomenal year," Manning said. "Making sacks, but also making a lot of tackles, just being around the football, knocking balls down, causing fumbles, getting safeties—he's all over the place."

The Drive

During the first 41 Super Bowls, only one game had ever featured a successful last-minute, come-from-behind touchdown drive. So history was not on quarterback Eli Manning's side when he led the Giants' offense onto the field in the last three minutes of Super Bowl XLII in February 2008, trailing the New England Patriots 14–10. The Giants made two first downs, then the drive nearly stalled out. On a tense fourth-down-and-one play, halfback Brandon Jacobs bulled through Patriots defenders for a crucial first down. Three plays later, Manning narrowly avoided being sacked and then heaved a 32-yard pass to receiver David Tyree, who leaped up, pinned the ball against his helmet, and somehow hung on to it for dear life. Giants players on the sidelines were now certain that their team would win and began chanting "17–14" to each other, predicting the final score. Four plays later, their prediction became reality when Manning connected with receiver Plaxico Burress for the winning touchdown. For days, New York sportswriters and fans debated what to name the Giants' amazing victory charge. Finally, they decided to call it simply "The Drive."

USING HIS HEAD, DAVID TYREE MADE A MEMORABLE SUPER BOWL CATCH

SPEEDSTER VICTOR CRUZ GAVE THE GIANTS' OFFENSE A DEEP THREAT

DEFENDERS (L-R) AARON BOSS, ANTONIO PIERCE, AND JAMES BUTLER

So were the 2011 Giants. After a 6–2 start, the team lost five of the next six. Wins in the two final games gave the Giants the NFC East title and some momentum going into the playoffs. They rode that momentum to defeat the Atlanta Falcons 24–2 and top-seeded Packers 37–20 in the first two rounds, then they eked out a 20–17 overtime win over San Francisco to advance to Super Bowl XLVI against New England. New York led 9–0 in the first quarter, but the Patriots scored 17 points that went unanswered until a pair of Giants field goals then narrowed the margin to 17–15 as the game entered the final quarter. Starting on his own 12-yard line with less than 4 minutes remaining, Manning engineered the game-winning drive in under 3 minutes, with the highlight being a seemingly miraculous pass to wide receiver Mario Manningham. What happened next, though, was one of the most bizarre touchdowns in Super Bowl history.

When Bradshaw took the handoff, the Giants were positioned at second and goal on the Patriots' six-yard line with 1:06 remaining. New York wanted to score, of course, but it also wanted to chew up as much time as possible before doing so. The Patriots, meanwhile, had apparently decided on a bold strategy of allowing New York to gain a touchdown, with the aim of getting the ball back in enough time to score themselves. Bradshaw ran unimpeded down the field but tried to stop at the one-yard line and force the Patriots to use their final timeout. However, sheer momentum carried him into the end zone. New England's quarterback Tom Brady then got his team as far as midfield, but a final "Hail Mary" pass fell incomplete, and the Giants declared victory.

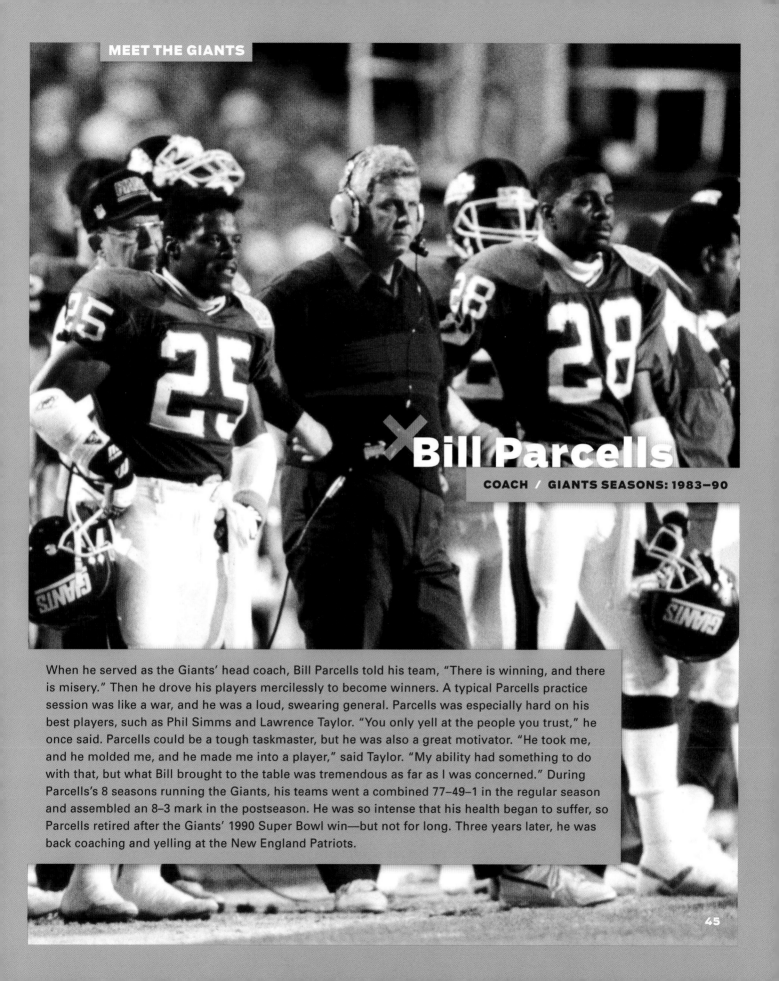

Bill Parcells

COACH / GIANTS SEASONS: 1983–90

When he served as the Giants' head coach, Bill Parcells told his team, "There is winning, and there is misery." Then he drove his players mercilessly to become winners. A typical Parcells practice session was like a war, and he was a loud, swearing general. Parcells was especially hard on his best players, such as Phil Simms and Lawrence Taylor. "You only yell at the people you trust," he once said. Parcells could be a tough taskmaster, but he was also a great motivator. "He took me, and he molded me, and he made me into a player," said Taylor. "My ability had something to do with that, but what Bill brought to the table was tremendous as far as I was concerned." During Parcells's 8 seasons running the Giants, his teams went a combined 77–49–1 in the regular season and assembled an 8–3 mark in the postseason. He was so intense that his health began to suffer, so Parcells retired after the Giants' 1990 Super Bowl win—but not for long. Three years later, he was back coaching and yelling at the New England Patriots.

TWO-TIME SUPER BOWL MVP ELI MANNING DID NOT REST ON HIS LAURELS

MARIO MANNINGHAM MADE A KEY SIDELINE CATCH IN SUPER BOWL XLVI

The Giants opened the 2012 season with every intention of defending their Super Bowl title. They lost only two of their first eight games, but the rigors of facing the NFL's toughest schedule (their opponents had a collective .547 winning percentage in 2011) soon caught up with them. A 33–14 thumping by the Ravens in the next-to-last game of the season dropped New York to 8–7. Even though the Giants beat the rival Eagles 42–14 in the 2012 finale, it wasn't enough to extend their play into the postseason.

ith four Super Bowl titles and another four NFL crowns from the pre-Super Bowl era, the Giants are among the most successful franchises in league history. Almost a century ago, Tim Mara had no way of knowing how much of a return his $500 initial investment would generate. The New York club's founding father would certainly be proud of the way the hundreds of players who have since called themselves Giants have represented the nation's largest city.

INDEX